Foothold on a Hillside

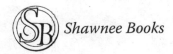 *Shawnee Books*

Foothold on a Hillside

Memories of a Southern Illinoisan

CHARLESS CARAWAY

Foreword by Paul Simon

SOUTHERN ILLINOIS UNIVERSITY PRESS
Carbondale

Copyright © 1986 by the Board of Trustees,
Southern Illinois University
Printed in the United States of America
20   19   18   17   6   5   4   3

Library of Congress Cataloging-in-Publication Data
     Caraway, Charless, 1888–1977.
     Foothold on a hillside.

     (Shawnee books)
     1. Caraway, Charless, 1888–1977. 2. Illinois—Biography.
3. Illinois—Social life and customs.
     I. Title.   II. Series.
     CT275.C2797A33 1986   977.3'04'0924   85-30381
     ISBN 0-8093-1297-2
     ISBN 0-8093-1298-0 (pbk.)

Printed on recycled paper. ♻

Contents

Contents

Contents

Illustrations

Foreword

There are two types of history. One relates the interplay of leaders and great events; our children read and discuss this type of history during their years in grade school, high school, and college. The second is the personal recollection, which gives us a flavor of the times and an insight into our heritage that the traditional history does not give.

Charless Caraway has provided us with the second type of history. And this type is no less important than the first.

Only a few of our citizens will have their personal histories published, but many ought to be sitting down and recalling the days of their youth and the events that helped to mold their lives. And this information ought to be part of a collection in every college and university library, every high school library, every community library, and every historical museum.

Charless Caraway's recollections enrich our understanding of where we have been. My hope is that his example will be followed by many others.

Paul Simon

Charless Caraway (1888–1977)

Preface

I sometimes hold it half a sin
  To put in words the grief I feel;
  For words, like Nature, half reveal
And half conceal the Soul within.
  —Tennyson, *In Memoriam*

In a last letter to Mom after her death in 1963, Dad wrote, "My life came crashing down about me." During the long, lonely months when he was struggling back to life (and recuperating from delayed cataract surgery), I often listened to the stories he loved to tell. Uproariously funny and poignant stories. Stories of personal loss and gain. Nostalgic stories of real people. His story. And every word was true. I told him one day that these authentic bits of history should not be lost to the future or reserved for an appreciative family—that he should have a much wider audience. So Dad began his writing "career" at the age of seventy-five ("Grandma Moses was a piker," he said). Each week I would collect another small segment. Finally, we had a manuscript! After we added old family photographs and other appropriate illustrations, it was ready for limited distribution.

At first Dad was very apprehensive about letting other than family members pore over his life story, but the response over a period of time from all who read it was more than encouraging. A unique flavor, a charm, a sincerity captivated his readers. They began to demand copies. Tentative steps toward publication began when Dad was a sturdy and spirited eighty-seven years old. The goal, of course, was to complete the process as soon as possible and let him experience the joy of seeing his words in print. He said, even then, that he did not expect to live to see the book published, though I know he harbored a faint hope. But time and other sorrows—the loss of two of his sons, Wayne in 1971 and Lester in 1974—had taken a toll.

On July 13, 1977, after a brief but devastating illness, Dad passed away. He fought a good fight to the very end. We are comforted to know that his strength and courage and humor, his remarkable stability in an unstable world, and all his other uncommon attributes (though he would scoff heartily at the very thought that his stories reveal any such personal qualities) will live in FOOTHOLD ON A HILLSIDE. Still, grief lingers. But he would not like that. I can just hear him saying gently but firmly, "You're looking at this thing in the wrong light. You need to think about something else. There's a story I've been meaning to tell you . . . and every word is true."

Cleo Caraway
Carbondale, Illinois

Acknowledgments

A number of the old photographs featured in this book are cherished family possessions. Others were contributed by interested area friends and neighbors. Rick Pease furnished the early photograph of Southern Illinois fruit pickers. Robert Stokes, University Photographer (Emeritus), Southern Illinois University at Carbondale, furnished the 1893 photograph of Southern Illinois Normal University (Old Main). The early photographs of the Illinois Central Railroad passenger house and of the division office and grounds at Carbondale were furnished by the Illinois Central Gulf Railroad. The 1905 photograph of the Murphysboro Street Railway was furnished by Rex Franklin; Martin Seibel furnished some details for the caption.

The turn-of-the-century photographs of Makanda were taken from the production of a documentary film entitled CHANGING TRACKS (copyright 1976, Richard Pease). Rick produced the film as a senior in Cinema and Photography at SIUC and spent many an hour searching the University Archives and visiting elderly residents of Makanda to obtain these photographs. F. A. Heern provided some of the interesting details in the captions.

Stricklin Studio of Eldorado furnished the photograph of Union Station in Eldorado. Julia Mitchell Etherton furnished the picture of the original home of the First National Bank and Trust Company in Carbondale. The Sharon School group picture was contributed by Lena Doody. Verda Sherwood Lambert provided the old photograph of the Sherwood home in Etherton Switch; caption detail was furnished by Verda, Mary Sauer, and Kathryn Moniger Boucher.

Dr. Robert Mohlenbrock, Professor Emeritus, Department of Botany, SIUC, contributed his illustrations of Southern Illinois medicinal plants. And Merlien W. King, former Supervisor of Graphics Design, University Publications and Graphic Services, SIUC, provided the illustration of log cabin construction and the map of Southern Illinois.

The plat map is an excerpt from the Triennial Atlas & Plat Book, Jackson County, Illinois, courtesy of the Rockford Map Publishers, Inc., Rockford, Illinois (copyright 1968).

Dates and other detailed information throughout the book were graciously verified by employees of SIUC's Morris Library, the Carbondale Public Library, and the Sallie Logan Public Library of Murphysboro.

Introduction

CHARLESS CARAWAY

In the winter of 1860, before the War between the States was upon them, the William P. Caraway family and the Thomas Powell family—though they were not acquainted with each other—joined the same group of people leaving Tennessee for Southern Illinois. These people were against secession from the Union. Thomas Powell was a man of considerable means. He had converted his monetary savings to gold, and it had been promptly confiscated by the Confederate government. Both families had to sell their farms in Tennessee quickly and at considerable financial loss in order to get out while they could. With the money they got for their land and surplus stock, they were able to buy land and settle as neighbors near Eldorado in Saline County, Illinois—the Powells in the uplands and the Caraways in the lowlands. William P. and Mary Jane Clemmons Caraway were the parents of seven children: Sarah Frances, William Riley, John James, Merritt M., Demaris Lunday, Tennessee Johnson, and Mary Jane. Thomas and Betty Sneed Powell were also the parents of seven children: Melvina, Martin, Fenton, George, Mary, Susan, and Annie.

Merritt Caraway and Melvina Powell both had been born in Wilson County, Tennessee, before their parents moved to Illinois. In 1877 they were married. I, their only son, was born to them November 20, 1888. On February 23, 1910, I married Bessie Mae Rowan, and we too became the parents of seven children; Lester, George, Wayne, Ethel, Cleo, Charley, and Betty Lou.

The following events of my life and time were set down as my personal offering to my ever-increasing family and to the interested of today's generations and those to come.

◪ Backwoods Tales   1

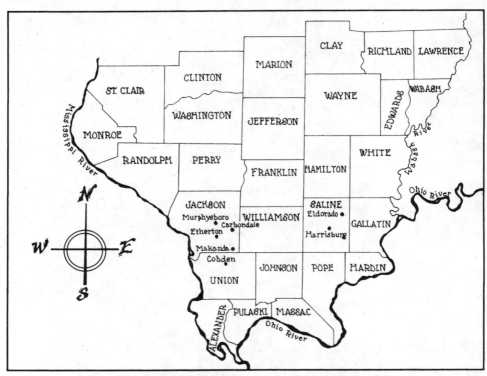

SOUTHERN ILLINOIS

Early to Bed

The night was cold, and there was a big fire going in the stick-and-mud fireplace. Dad suddenly realized that some of the dirt had fallen off, leaving the sticks exposed, and that the chimney itself was on fire. There was just one thing to do. He put a long pole between the chimney and the house and pried the chimney over, and it fell out in the yard. You can imagine what kind of a mess we were in—we had to go to bed to keep from freezing. As soon as they could, Dad and some of the neighbors rebuilt the chimney, and we were all back to normal again. This, one of my earliest memories, happened when I was about three years old and we lived in a one-room log cabin with a lean-to kitchen on the Bennett place near Eldorado in Saline County, Illinois. It wasn't an unusual occurrence—as a matter of fact, it happened every now and then.

Homesteading and Housewarming

In the late 1800s there were still large tracts of timberland in Saline County. Quite a number of people depended on this land and its timber for their living. Many of them were homesteaders. A man would take a ten-year lease on ten acres. There would be nothing on the acreage but

SINGLE-BIT AXE
used for felling trees

(Offset handle and cutting edge on one side only)

BROAD AXE
used for squaring logs

FROE
used with mallet for splitting clapboards from blocks of wood

1. Felled tree was limbed and log cut to proper length.

2. Log was stripped of bark and 'twanged with Squaring Cord.

3. Deep vertical cuts were then made along chalk line with long-handled Felling Axe.

4. Final smooth hewing was done with chiseled side of Broad Axe out and left knee close to log.

5. End-notched logs were laid up to form walls. Clapboard roof completed exterior of standard log cabin.

Steps in log cabin construction

trees and, of course, underbrush. The homesteader would agree to clear the land and put it under the plow during the period of his lease. He had to be an expert woodsman and especially good with an axe, a broad axe, and a froe. With these tools he built his house. He felled the trees, cut them into proper lengths, and hewed them into proper shape, notching the logs at each corner so as to make them fit neatly and snugly together. He would rive out long pieces for the rafters and for the strips to fasten the clapboards to. Then came the clapboards themselves. These he made from blocks of wood, riving them out with a froe. Pickets or palings for the yard fence were made the same way. Puncheons for the floor were split from large logs and hewn down to something near uniform thickness. A loft wasn't considered important until some of the youngsters were big enough to climb the wall. Then the homesteader might lay some more puncheons and set some pegs in the wall for the children to climb. The stick-and-mud fireplace finished the home. The hearth and jambs, of course, were all dirt. The heat and smoke of the fireplace flavored this dirt so that sometimes children would eat it and almost become addicted to it, refusing to eat anything else.

After all this work was done, a housewarming was in order. All the fiddlers for miles around would come and bring their fiddles. Naturally, this frolic took place outside; there wasn't room in the house for anything like that. That old hard cider was rather slow, but it never quit. Things would be quiet and peaceful-like for some time, but sooner or later something just had to happen. It generally started over one thing: someone who couldn't hold his liquor very well would make a slighting remark about somebody's girl or his coon dog. That was all it took to start a regular knock-down, drag-out fight. The next day everything was back to normal—the best man won, and there were no grudges. Of course, there would be quite a few toenails lying around the clearing—this freshly cleared land, with all the stumps and snags, was rough on those who weren't wearing shoes!

A Good Day's Work

Since much of the land in Saline County was still forested in the late 1800s, many men made their living from working in the woods. Railroad ties were ready sale. The tie makers were rugged men. They had to swing an axe from sunup to sundown and come back the next day and do the same thing (try that sometime).

Ten ties were considered a good day's work for one man. He would take an axe and a broad axe, a maul and wedges, a crosscut saw, and a gallon or so of strong coffee with him to the woods. First, he would build a small fire to keep the coffee hot. Then he would proceed to chop down a big tree that was to be made into ties. The end of the log had to be sawn off to even it up so the ties would be uniform in size. Then he would saw the huge log into eight-foot sections and split the sections with the maul and wedges into pieces as near to the size and shape of a tie as he could get them. Finally, he would use the axe and broad axe to chop and hew the sections into the finished ties.

I remember my father telling about a man who hired someone to cut ties for him. The hired hand thought he had done a good day's work and told his boss in the evening that he had made ten ties that day. The man told him that was all right for the first day but to try to make eleven the next day. The hired hand just up and "knocked his block off" and went looking for another job! That didn't change a thing, of course, but the people around there did get a kick out of it.

High Adventure

Ours was a backwoods area. It took a day to travel by team and wagon to and from Eldorado, so we went there only when it was absolutely necessary to get supplies. Once, when I was about four, my father and I arrived just in time to see a runaway team pulling a wagon down through town. The wagon broke up when it was thrown against a tree, and the horses finally stopped. That was one of the most exciting experiences of my young life!

My mother rarely went to town. I remember her saying that there was a ten-year period in her life when her children were coming along (she had six children, including twins, and lost three of them) that she never went to town. But she didn't feel that hers was a hard lot. She did her job as she saw it and was perfectly happy. She always had time for us and a knack for making ordinary things seem special. When I was still a very small lad, she sat me on her knee and taught me how to whistle. I progressed in short order from puckering and blowing to whistling a pretty good tune. Then she taught me how to sing. My father, in his

The Murray School group picture taken in 1894, when the author and his family lived in Rector Bottoms. Charless (six years old) is fourth from left in the first row. Sisters Emma and Ella (eight and ten years old) are first and second from right in the third row. The adults in the last row are parents who came to be photographed (this was a custom at that time). The author's father is second from left, and his mother and aunt are first and second from right.

younger days, had a beautiful singing voice. Sometimes my mother and father and my two sisters and I joined others in community sings at church or in the homes. We knew all the folk songs that were popular then, like "Barbara Allen" and "The Maple on the Hill," and the old hymns. I still know the words to some of them.

I remember the day my father decided I was old enough for a venture of my own and fixed me up with a fishing pole and let me go down to the creek to fish. Even young children (I was about five years old at the time) were expected to act like adults in those days, so my parents weren't worried that I would fall in the creek and drown or anything like that. Soon, I caught me a fish! I was so excited I didn't take it off the hook. As fast as I could run, I took fish, hook, line, and pole home. My father and mother were standing in the yard talking to Old Man Mars, a medicine man who lived about a quarter of a mile from us and came by our place to take in corn from the creek bottoms. I was trembling from head to toe. I asked my mother why I was shaking so. Old Man Mars said, "You ain't the first one that ever done that, Sonny. Don't worry about it."

My mother showed me how to clean my little catfish and then fried it for me.

Trading Down to Rector Bottoms

My father was quite a trader. We didn't stay on the Bennett place long. Dad soon bought the McGee place, a twenty-acre triangular plot formed where the railroad cut across a forty diagonally. We stayed there about a year. Then we settled on the Litschler place, smack in the middle of Rector Bottoms (in the valley of Rector Creek in Saline County). This was about nine miles north of Eldorado in the Murray School District. It looked as if we'd hit the jackpot at last—forty acres of as fine a land as a crow ever flew over. We found out later—almost too much later—that that was about all it was fit for. This bottomland wasn't too bad for creatures who could fly or climb trees or breathe under water, but for us poor earthbound souls it was very bad.

There was no high ground near. The house was built on wood blocks that were supposed to keep you out of water. When it was necessary to go out, you just had to wade through ankle-deep muck. In places it might be up to a man's pockets—in that case he simply moved his chewing tobacco up to a drier place and went on with the chores. Dad kept a long piece of timber stuck down in the well so we could tell where it was and not step off into it when the water was up. When the water had gone down, the well was left full of overflow water. After a few days it would ferment and have a head on it like a freshly drawn glass of beer. We couldn't use water like that, of course, so Mother would send us kids down to the slough for some fresh water. If it was summertime, we would hit the water a few times with the dipper to warn the tadpoles to get out of there—as I recall, some of them had legs already.

I'm sure you've concluded by now that this was not the healthiest place in the world to live. The fact is, we all very nearly died. We had the second- or third-day chills (I hope you *don't* know what that means). Dad had a bone felon on his thumb, and the bone came out. Mother had erysipelas in one side of her face and almost died.

Dad did have one good harvest before we all fell ill. This "made" land, or "new ground," produced a wilderness of corn, sorghum cane, and tobacco and all the wheat, hay, and garden stuff we could use. The finest ears of corn were hand-picked and hand-shelled for meal, and the wheat was threshed for flour. Tobacco was a good cash crop.

Potions and Notions

Keeping healthy in the backwoods of Saline County *was* a challenge. And sometimes the cure was worse than the affliction. I'm thinking now of the practice of hanging asafetida bags around the necks of children to ward off diseases. The heat of the body would melt it down into a gooey, foul-smelling mess that would almost kill you. But the old folks thought it had to be done, so you did it. If the asafetida bag didn't work, though, a number of home remedies were commonly used.

Sulphur, I recall, was used as a purifier for our systems in the spring of the year. It was mixed with sorghum molasses into a nauseating dose that generally took two adults to administer. One would pull the child's head back with one hand and hold the nose with the other, and someone else would pour the mixture down the throat. The child had two choices: swallow it, or choke to death!

Red sassafras tea was also taken in the spring to purify and thin the blood for hot weather.

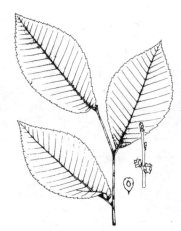

Red sassafras (*Sassafras albidum*)   Slippery elm (*Ulmus rubra*)

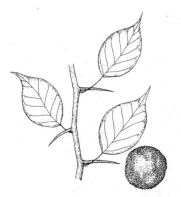

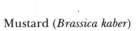

Mayapple (*Podophyllum peltatum*):   Hedgeapple (*Maclura pomifera*)   Mustard (*Brassica kaber*)
branch and fruit

Quinine came in powder form and was used for malaria, of course. But getting it down a sick child was a problem that called for some ingenuity. About one-half inch of the thick outer bark of slippery elm was hewn off to reach the inner bark. The pale-yellow inner bark was cut in strips about six to eight inches long. Several pieces were put into a glass of water. Overnight, mucus would form on the strips. A tablespoonful of the mucus wrapped around the powdered quinine made a good dose. Adults mixed their quinine in whiskey and took it morning and night.

Mullein, a cabbage-like plant, was gathered and stored in a dry place to make mullein tea, which was used for lung and throat trouble.

Life everlasting, a white-blooming weed, was gathered in the fields and stored in a dry place. In the winter if you got a cold, you ground up the bloom and smoked it in a pipe to break up congestion.

A white-topped meadow weed was used for intestinal trouble. This particular plant grows in hay fields. It is a slim weed about four feet high, with a square stem about the size of a pencil. The last eight to ten inches of the stem is tender and juicy. After peeling, you simply ate the center of the weed.

I'm sure you've heard of mustard plasters. Mustard seeds were crushed and mixed with vinegar to make a paste for relieving pain.

For rheumatism, large ears of corn were boiled in their husks until they were steaming through and through. Then they were wrapped securely and placed on the affected parts until the pain was gone.

Mayapple roots were boiled and pounded into a mush to make a drawing poultice for man or beast.

A heated solution of vinegar and salt was used for a sprained ankle. The solution was poured over brown paper which was then wrapped in layers and tied around the ankle until it was better.

The stems of wild touch-me-nots were crushed to get juice to smear on poison-ivy rash.

Hedgeapple juice was used to get rid of warts.

Saline County people were famous for their good teeth and sound gums. They took charcoal right out of ashtrays, ground it up into a fine powder, and mixed it with baking soda and salt to be applied with the fingers for their teeth. Red corncobs were burned in a vessel, and the ash was used for sound gums.

Have you ever wondered what the backwoodsman used for shoe

polish? An excellent black shoe polish was made by turning a cap on the cookstove bottom side up and mixing the whites of two eggs with the soot.

So much for potions and notions. There were many others, of course. These few came easily to mind, and some of them might better have been forgotten.

Profile of a Backwoodsman

Rector Bottoms was very sparsely settled in the late 1800s. There were clearings here and there, but for the most part the land was taken up by almost untouched forest. The people who lived there were real back-woodsmen. They knew nothing of city life or the ways of city people, and I might add they were not anxious to learn about such things. One of these backwoodsmen made a lasting impression on me as a small and very curious boy. I don't recall his real name—everyone called him "Bucky."

Bucky was quite a man to see when he was fully dressed with his squirrel-skin cap, cowhide boots, heavy jean pants and coat, and an old hickory shirt. He owned a small piece of land on one of the creeks that flowed into Rector. He didn't do much farming himself, but his son and wife did what they could to grow some garden stuff and the like.

Bucky had other irons in the fire. He was a peddler, a hunter, a fisherman, a trapper, a handyman, and a part-time preacher. He patched pots and pans and sharpened scissors and knives. He sold pills, pins and needles, shoe nails, buttons, thread, matches, bits of ribbon and lace, and small cans of brick dust to the folks in the settlement.

The brick dust was made by simply pounding yellow bricks into a fine powder. Coal oil was just coming into use, and everyone was scared stiff that it would blow up. Bucky was nobody's fool. He set himself up in the brick dust business, and he had no competition. He claimed his brick dust would prevent the terrible explosion that everyone feared, and he would "prove" his point by putting some coal oil in a cup and sprinkling a little of the mysterious dust into it. Then he would strike a match and put it out by plunging it into the oil. This demonstration was quite convincing to these uninformed people, and Bucky went to great lengths to warn them never to use coal oil without the dust. He also warned his customers not to accept any substitutes which could, and probably would, "blow them to pieces."

As Bucky went about his "work," he took along things that he would most likely need. Like his faithful Airedale dog, Ol' Stub (his tail was about four inches long). Ol' Stub was a good hunter and would track or tree any kind of game day or night. He was big and mean and dedicated to the idea of protecting Bucky and his property. Bucky's property included a double-barreled muzzle-loading shotgun, shot pouch, a game bag, and the things he sold. This man made quite a picture as he came striding through the forest with all the tools of his trade and his great dog at heel. As Bucky and Ol' Stub went from place to place, they were always on the lookout for game. Sometimes on Sundays Bucky would go by the meeting house. In that case he would leave his gun and dog and game at the edge of the clearing. If the occasion demanded, he would deliver the sermon. He didn't have to worry about the things he left in care of Ol' Stub.

One Sunday morning when Bucky arrived at the meeting house, a testimonial service was in progress. Everyone was to stand up and give praise to the Lord for His goodness and thank Him for all the things they had received. When it came Bucky's time, he stood up to his full height (which, by the way, was about five feet two, boots and all) and said in a loud, clear voice, "Ladies and gentlemen, I owe my life to my dog and gun, Rector Bottoms, and cathartic pills." I don't think anyone ever did figure out just where the Lord came in.

Bucky was a man to be remembered.

A Family Circus

Late in the fall of 1894, when we were still living in Rector Bottoms, a family of people and a six-hundred-pound bear made their winter camp in a wooded area near the creek about one-quarter of a mile from our place. Maybe you can imagine the excitement this stirred up in that backwoods region, but I doubt it. There were four in the family: the parents, and a boy and a girl about nine and ten years old. They were performers, and so was the bear. They held circus shows all winter for the local people. The children would do their song-and-dance act barefoot, and the only visible clothing they wore was a sort of nightshirt. They ran races barefoot over the frozen ground and gathered nuts, wild grapes, papaws, and acorns from the chinquapin oaks in the woods. When these acorns were roasted, they weren't bad at all and were quite nourishing.

The family's tent was barely large enough to sleep four, so they had no place to build a fire inside. All they had in the way of heat or light was a lantern hung overhead. They gathered leaves to make their mattresses, and then they covered the mattresses with such as they had. The pillows were feed sacks stuffed with more leaves.

The bear was rather good at making his bed. When the weather got bad, he would rake up a big pile of leaves and crawl under them and take a long nap. Then he would come out and sit in the family circle around the open fire. He would lock his front and hind paws together and rock back and forth while warming the bottoms of his feet. He would eat thirty or forty big ears of corn just about any time—he ate it off the cob like a hog. For our entertainment, his trainer would have him climb one of the big trees. He didn't like to do this, but when the man started cursing him in some kind of foreign language, he would go on up. He tested each limb by taking hold of it with his front paw. If he could break it off, he would throw it to the ground and go up to the next one. The man and the bear would wrestle once in a while, but that was special.

Of course, everyone took something when they went to see the show, which was quite often. This was the way the family made their living. They depended entirely on the people for their food and clothing, such as it was, and seemed to be content and very healthy. They didn't have colds or other ailments, and their appetites seemed to be perfect. For the most part, they ate corn bread, homemade hominy, sorghum, turnips, beans, a few scraps of salt pork, a few onions and salt-saucered pickles, and what they had been able to gather from the forests and fields.

And so the winter of 1894–95 passed on into history—at least it was history for me! One fine day in March, the family loaded what few things they had into their one-horse wagon and went on their way. This was their way of life. We missed them for a while.

On Higher Ground

Poor Dad, he finally had to give up on the Litschler place—he owned forty acres of the best land in the state and couldn't live on it. He took off one morning to find us a healthier place to live. And he found it—a big, fine log house on Aunt Kara Scozier's place with a large stone-and-brick fireplace, complete with firedogs and pothooks. It was up on high ground in the Greenhill School District, about two miles from our former home. There was no malaria there, and we moved in and settled down to regain our health and strength. We had been there for about six weeks and were just beginning to perk up a bit when Uncle George Powell came up from southeast Missouri where he had been working. He was to stay with us that winter. Unfortunately, he had been there only a short time when he came down with the measles. Of course, we all had them, except for Dad; he just had a very bad case of the grippe (we call it the flu now). There were five of us down at the same time. Dad did manage to stay up and sort of look after the rest of us. Uncle George and mother were very sick—it began to look as if they might not make it, but they did. After about a month of this we were all able to sit up and take nourishment. We finally made it through the winter, and our dear departed relative was just a memory and not such a fond one at that.

The Scozier place was a temporary home. Soon, Dad sold his Rector Bottom forty and bought twenty acres in the Shiloh School District from Uncle John Caraway. There was no house on this land, so we lived in a small tenant house on the David Harris place about one-quarter of a mile away until Dad could get a house built for us.

Uncle John and his two sons were operating the Carlyle Sawmill near their home at that time. This was a large mill, and there were several hired hands. The site had enough buildings to house all the help, and it was called "Mill Town." It was right beside what is now U.S. Route 45, about four miles north of Eldorado en route to Carmi. Oxen were used to bring the logs in from the woods. They had their own special pen where they were fed corn and hay, and it included part of the mill pond where they watered. The oxen were well-kept animals. They had to be shod like horses. Oxen, of course, have split hooves and had to have two shoes on each foot. They didn't take kindly to shoeing and had to be thrown in order to get the job done. This was no easy chore! The tips of their horns were trimmed down, and brass knobs were screwed into the horns, with tassels sometimes attached. I recall seeing huge loads of logs being brought out of Rector Bottoms on ox-drawn wagons. The riders atop the loads had whips but no lines.

There were two other such sawmills within a ten-mile radius of that area. Dad made the lumber deal for our new house with the owner of one of the other mills because he delivered his product. All the lumber for the framing came in one dray load pulled by a team of two massive

The author's father, Merritt M. Caraway, at nineteen. This photograph is a copy of an 1875 tintype.

draft horses weighing close to a ton each. These horses—Clydesdales or Percherons, most likely—were famous in the area and hauled all the lumber for this mill. We were on the building site when they arrived, and you can imagine the impressions they made on a seven-year-old boy. I'll never forget it. Dad and a buddy built our small house—two rooms with a lean-to kitchen—in no time. Dad was knocked unconscious and almost killed when a heavy piece of lumber fell on his head during the construction. But he recovered. Pound for pound, my father was one of the toughest men I have ever known.

On Higher Ground

◈ Makanda Life   2

The Move to Jackson County

We lived in our new house for about a year, but the crop was not good and times were hard. Some of our neighbors who had been to Jackson County came back and told Dad about the fine ridge farming land that lay from south of Carbondale to Cobden—the heart of the fruit and vegetable growing region—and that men, women, and children were being hired to work in the fields and orchards. So Dad decided to move to Jackson County where we could all work. Previously we had moved from one place to another within a settlement or from one settlement to the next, all within the vicinity of Eldorado. Now we were going a considerable distance—and no previous arrangements had been made. Our neighbor, Willis Cox, who had been to the area before, moved us in March 1896. He had a big, fine team of horses and a covered wagon. The John Wiley farm, one of the largest and best-known farms in the area, was our destination. We would go southwest from Eldorado to Harrisburg, due west to Carbondale, and south to Makanda. These were all dirt roads then, of course.

My sisters and I had never seen hills and valleys such as we were to travel. We rode in the wagon sometimes but walked most of the time and led the cow. As we climbed our first real hill, we were afraid—we didn't know what would happen to us when we reached the top!

This was a three-day trip. At night we cooked bacon and coffee and little else over a campfire. Mother slept in the wagon, but the rest of us slept under the stars. I took my blanket and curled up under the

When the author and his family traveled through Carbondale in March 1896 by covered wagon on their way to Makanda, the Illinois Central Railroad station house looked like this. They never dreamed at the time that a few years later they would be making the same journey by train.

wagon, with a corner of the blanket tucked under my head for a pillow. The weather was fine for March, but the nights were cool.

We stopped the wagon in Carbondale to look at Southern Illinois Normal University. There was only one building on the campus at that time, and it was a most imposing structure with beautiful grounds. We had never seen anything like it (you must remember that Eldorado was a very small country town at that time).

As we left Carbondale, we came upon a little stream with clear, cold water flowing over a bed of rocks and pretty pebbles. We children had never seen anything like it, either. We stopped again and got a drink and wondered at this new land we had entered.

This lovely little park, with its fountain and bandstand, greeted Illinois Central Railroad passengers at Carbondale in a more genteel era. In the summer of 1905, when the author and his parents were living on the Old McKinnon farm near Makanda, he came to Carbondale to visit Ella, one of his married sisters, and saw the first all-weather road being laid in the city. He watched as men shoveled gravel out of boxcars parked in the Illinois Central freight yard, moved it in wheelbarrows up a steep platform to dump it into a large mixer, and hauled the gravel-cement mixture in horse-drawn dump wagons to the street they were paving. It was a very impressive operation.

We were taken right to the door of John Wiley's house, near Makanda. Mr. Wiley had just hired a man, but he liked the looks of our family and arranged for us to stay in his tenant house nearby until we could find a steady job: A widow and her two children were living there temporarily, but it was a large house and there was room for all of us.

Soon we found a job on the Bob Miller place. His tenant house was empty, and we moved right in. "Uncle Bob" (we were taught as small children to refer to older people as Uncle or Aunt or Grandpa or Grandma) was in his sixties and had long white hair and sideburns and chin whis-

Southern Illinois Normal University (the Old Main Building) as seen by the author and his family when they passed through Carbondale in March 1896 on their way to Makanda.

kers that almost reached his waistband. He was the first one in that settlement to own a graphinola with a horn, and he was very proud of it. Sometimes, on rare Sunday afternoons, he invited us over to listen to his records. We dressed in our Sunday best and sat stiffly in his parlor and knew that we were privileged indeed.

We hadn't been in Makanda long when Dad sold his twenty acres in Saline County for six hundred dollars. So there he was—a rich man at last. Six hundred dollars cash in his pocket, we all had a steady job, and we had one of the finest and best milk cows that ever was. "Old Pied," we called her. She was yellow with white patches and so gentle that all three of us kids could milk her at the same time. She seemed to really enjoy it. She would stand perfectly still with her ears flopped down and her eyes half-closed and chew her cud as only a contented cow can. But this was too good to last, of course. Old Pied ate a bellyful of white clover one morning while the dew was on. She became bloated and was dead before night. So once again the roof caved in on us. Now this may seem silly to you, but we loved that cow. Dad paid a man to take her over on his farm to bury her, and made him promise not to mutilate her in any way in the process. Although this was a devastating calamity to us, we did survive it. Dad bought another cow, and we were all right again.

The Good Old Days

As I mentioned earlier, we moved to the Makanda area so we could all work. We worked at the Bob Miller farm for one season. Then we moved back to the tenant house on the John Wiley farm, where we worked for about two seasons. After that we moved on to the Dick Ellis farm. There were all kinds of fruits and vegetables to be grown and harvested. My father, my mother, my two sisters, and I worked in the fields and orchards. Father received seventy-five cents a day and Mother got fifty cents a day. The girls were older than I and got forty cents. My daily wage was twenty-five cents. And just to keep the record straight, a day's work was from sunrise to sunset—and that didn't mean just setting behind a cloud, either. So, if we all worked six full days, which we usually did, we had $13.80 coming. This huge sum was not paid out freely. In fact, the actual payment wasn't made until the boss had given quite a lengthy speech on the proper use and handling of considerable wealth. This took place every Sunday morning. You see, we did the boss's chores on Sunday, too. No. there was no pay for that, but the week was finally finished. Well, almost—we came back Sunday evenings and did the chores again.

Ours wasn't an isolated case. Back then, that was the accepted way of life for hired hands in Jackson County. That's what we were in those

These Southern Illinois fruit pickers were from the Anna area about twelve miles south of Makanda. Men, women, and children worked in the fields and orchards from sunrise to sunset six days a week.

days—people who worked by the day for wages, if you can call what we got wages. Nothing was ever said about hours. And I almost forgot something. The men who worked on the farms in that area went to the barn with their lanterns each morning to care for the livestock and to feed, curry, and harness the teams that would be working that day. *Then* they returned home for breakfast. After breakfast everyone who was to work that day would go to the boss's place and wait, generally outside the entrance gate or maybe inside the tool shed if the weather was bad, for him to come out. We didn't wait long. Occasionally my father and I would get off at quartering time—that's what they called it, and it was four o'clock in the afternoon—to go to Makanda for groceries. Of course, we walked there and back, which was about two miles, and carried the next week's

The author (age ten) and his sister Emma (age twelve) had this picture taken at Makanda one day when their mother sent them to town with thirty cents to buy spoons. The store had no spoons, so they had the picture made instead.

supplies. The boss's mules and horses had been working very hard, you see, and they needed rest.

So these were the good old days you sometimes hear people raving about—generally people who didn't live in those times when a man worked for twelve or fourteen hours for seventy-five cents and paid fifteen cents a pound for bacon!

A Rockbound Metropolis

Makanda was quite a place in those days. I think the only thing Chicago had on Makanda was just that there was more of it. At its peak, the population was about three hundred and fifty. Some of the young people went away to work, but most of them stayed and earned their living in Makanda.

There was a lot of business in Makanda. A large amount of farm produce was shipped from the town, and there were stock pens for holding and loading livestock. It was a tank town, too. George Bell ran a restaurant where the train crews ate when the trains stopped for water. George and his wife and mother-in-law were well-liked, respected, and successful Negro members of the community, and the food in their restaurant was acknowledged to be the best for miles around. The women's specialty was apple pie, which was consumed in large quantities daily with gallons of hot, rich coffee. I also recall Makanda having a flour and feed mill, two blacksmith shops (one run by John Sill and the other by Tom Peak), D. F. Bennett's drugstore, two hotels (one called the Hopkins House and the other the Lense Place), a coffin shop where they made and sold coffins, a shoe shop where they made and repaired shoes, a bank, a post office, a cooper shop, a barber shop, a soda fountain, a butcher shop (where you could buy fresh meat if the butcher wasn't too drunk to wait on you), and usually five or six grocery stores. Two or three of these were what you might call general stores. And, oh yes, there was Old Man Drake, who carved tombstones from native rock.

All kinds of meetings, shows, and political gatherings were held in the upper story of the R. E. Bridges Building. It was there the Republican politicians made their wonderful speeches and warned us about all the terrible things that would happen if a Democrat should be elected. What few Democrats there were went into hiding until this business was finished. The most important ones, I recall, were Judge Willard J. Ellis and Isaac K. Levy. They were young men then and very prominent in Jackson County politics.

I remember one day when there was a terrible rain a few miles south of town. The runoff all came down Drury Creek, with Makanda squarely in its path. The water got several feet deep in the business part of town and washed away a good portion of the board sidewalks and some of the smaller buildings—including the five-by-five ones with loopholes in the sides, which had been put there by the early settlers as a means of defense against the Indians. The buildings didn't go very far until they lodged against some willows. When the water receded, the drayman dragged them back and put them up again. And so the old town soon was back to normal.

Any account of Makanda would have to mention what some, at least, considered the most important place in town—Bill Oldenhage's saloon. Can you imagine what happened to some of these poor souls when liquor was voted out? The oasis suddenly dried up, and they were left floundering around in the hot, dry sand. Their eyes became glazed, their lips cracked, and their voices were a sort of dry croak, if they spoke at all. I'm sure they knew just how a poor fish feels when it is yanked out of the water and finds itself in the hot sun and the still hotter hand of its captor. These were really desperate people! They had kept their spirits wetted down for so long it had become second nature, and the suddenness of this dry spell was all but unbearable. Of course, they tried to figure something out, and they did come up with a fairly workable solution. They couldn't all go to Carbondale; they didn't have the money to spare; and besides, the little woman was watching like a hawk. So they cooked up a likely scheme. They would give their money to one or two who had more freedom of action, and the rest would wait at home. The next morning they would casually saunter uptown, and they usually came back feeling a little too frisky. Needless to say, this method of deception didn't work for long, but it was a good try.

A Rockbound Metropolis

But, believe it or not, these people were far more content than most people are today. They didn't "fall out" with heart attacks, as people do so often nowadays, nor did "men in white coats" come and take them away. They didn't have automobiles—neither their own nor the other fellow's—to worry about. Most people walked to church and Sunday school, or anywhere else they went. The young people would just start walking down the road, and others would join them along the way. Once in a while you would meet someone driving a team—that was all the traffic there was. Can you imagine the whole countryside being so quiet and peaceful?

This village, nestled between two high and rockbound hills and set astride Old Drury Creek, was my "hometown" from age seven to almost twenty-seven, and I will always love the memory of those years and that place.

A hillside view of Makanda in the early 1900s. Please see the notation by D. F. Bennett on the photograph. Bennett owned the drugstore in Makanda.

A closer view of Makanda by D. F. Bennett. Note the picturesque little Methodist church to the upper left.

A view west across the railroad tracks and through the telephone wires at Makanda. Note the double bridge—one side for pedestrians and one for wagons—across Drury Creek. The building next to the tracks on the right was the Bell Restaurant. The small building at its rear with a slanted roof was a pumphouse that kept the tank full of water for trains passing through Makanda. The old livery stable is visible between the restaurant and the pumphouse.

The Richard Ridgeway grocery store in the R. E. Bridges Building, which faced west on Main Street. Ridgeway, first on the left, was the son of the Richard Ridgeway pictured on page 39 with other Makanda residents. Charlie Watson, a part-time school teacher, is third from the left. This photograph was taken about 1912.

A close-up view of the bank and adjoining businesses in Makanda. The cooper shop is at the far left, and the store on the right sold hardware and lumber.

A busy freight yard at Makanda. Note the cars on the siding being loaded with produce from wagons while others waited to get in line, the cattle-loading ramp in the background, and the village well.

The old freight house at Makanda shown from the rear, with the hitchrack in the foreground, cars on the siding, and the freight shed on the left.

Makanda during a flood. This was not an unusual occurrence, since Drury Creek flowed right through the center of town. The first house on the right was the office of Frank Hopkins, justice of the peace. The large center building was Hopkins House, one of Makanda's two hotels. The fourth house from the right was the home of Dr. Lawrence Thompson.

The author remembers this as Bill Etherton's mill and house. The floodwaters were up. The lean-to room with the window on the left side of the mill was the engine room. One summer the author's father fired the engine, and the author, a young man then, would go to the mill and talk to his father at the window when he wasn't busy.

A funeral for a Civil War veteran in Makanda about 1905. Pictured (left to right) are John Sill, the village blacksmith; Frank Hopkins, postmaster, justice of the peace, and owner of Hopkins House; Will Fly, farmer; Frank Picquett; Charles Hamilton, police magistrate; William Goodwin (Civil War veteran); unidentified; Henry Short (Civil War veteran); unidentified; Richard Ridgeway, farmer and storeowner; and Marion Jackson, the Methodist preacher. The author recalls that several Civil War veterans lived very comfortably on their pensions (about seventy dollars a month) in this rural community.

A gathering of some of the male population of Makanda in the freight yard in 1911. Note D. F. Bennett's drugstore on the right. The man in the apron in the upper right-hand corner of the picture is George Bell, owner of the famous Bell Restaurant.

A Few Firsts

It was there in Makanda that I finally did see an automobile—the first one I'd ever seen, and the first for most other people of that community. Frank Sumner brought it down and parked it in front of his place of business in what was known as the Bell Building (Hod Bell kept a general store there for many years). All the farmers from back in the hills walked around it for about an hour, looking at it and wondering what made it go. Finally, one old man from way up the creek spat out a mouthful of tobacco juice and said in a very slow and solemn way, "Well, fellers, he got'er down here—now, let's see'm get'er out." I have often heard people remark about how solemn and tight-lipped these hillbilly farmers were and I think I can bring some light to bear on that subject. Did you ever try a great big smile with your mouth full of tobacco juice? You simply have to be tight-lipped until you can find a place to spit!

John Mulcaster was the station agent at Makanda at that time. Of course, he was pretty well up on the business of sending messages. The depot was a favorite loafing place for the men of that area. One day John was telling a group of them about how the railroad and others were considering a new way of sending messages without the use of wires. No one said anything, but they exchanged those knowing glances that are used on certain occasions and are quite effective. After John had gone inside, one old man who was considered by many to be well informed said, "It's too bad about Old John—his mind is completely gone." The others all agreed.

Quite a few of us saw our first movie in Makanda, and to the best of my knowledge it was the last one to be shown there. It was silent, of course, but it surely did shimmy around. We sat there with our eyes bugged out until it was over—it took almost an hour to get them shut again.

Local "Justice"

Yes, I think Makanda had everything that Chicago had and was just as tough—maybe tougher. When these people spoke their mind on some matter, they spoke it clearly and to the point. If you happened to see it differently, that was all right with them—but it was best not to push it. Mostly, they were solemn, serious-minded people, and I think it was generally accepted as fact that it was a paying proposition to mind your own business.

As I said before, Makanda had just about everything. Squire Hagler, a self-made man, as he said, had read law in his home and built up quite a reputation as a law man. He did plead quite a few cases in the Jackson County Court. He was very cunning and quite witty, and the local wrongdoers were very much aware of this. It was usually fairly quiet around town, but when some poor unfortunate was hauled before the justice of the peace, things really began to hum. Like the time the Widow Carter was brought into J.P. court for getting water from a neighbor's well after she'd been told not to. They fined her three dollars, and she refused to pay and walked out of the courtroom followed by her three rather husky daughters. The constable and his two deputies—they were the two blacksmiths mentioned earlier—rushed out to bring them back. They caught up with them and tried to surround them there in the street. There these four women stood, back to back and not saying a word. The constable had the reputation of being a brave man—well, he did have until this battle of the sexes, you might say. Anyway, he stepped right up and took hold of the arm of one of the daughters and said, "Come on, let's go." I think that was the last conscious moment he had for quite a spell. They went, all right. While three of the women were wrestling the constable, the fourth was taking the other men turnabout, jumping on their backs, clamping her legs firmly around their waists with one arm around their necks, and literally tearing at their eyeballs with her other hand. The other three weren't loafing on the job, either. But what really put the finishing touch to the fight was when one of the women got this two-hundred-and-forty-pound blacksmith, this mighty, brawny man, by the finger with her teeth and hung on and chewed like a bulldog. Well, he finally tore himself loose, and right then and there he decided that discretion *was* the better part of valor. He just stood there in the street, waving his hand in the air and yelling, "Somebody get the doctor—I've been bitten by a madwoman!" The others went to the aid of their wounded comrade, and the prisoners made their getaway. No one went after them. Then these three men, who had taken the oath to bring the wicked before the bar of justice and to protect the innocent, made their rather painful way to the doctor's office, where the tags of skin were clipped away and medication was applied. Quite a number of shin plasters were also in order—women's shoes were much more substantial then than now!

Summer Pastimes

For the most part the young people in Makanda, as elsewhere, had to make their own entertainment, and almost everything held promise. I recall a pastime that began when I was about sixteen years old and we were living on the Old McKinnon farm near Makanda. The Rock Springs School was about one hundred and fifty yards from our house, and John Miller's place was about two hundred yards from there. Other houses were all around, about one-quarter of a mile apart on small tracts of land. We had no telephones or any other means of direct communication. On summer evenings about dusk we sat in our yards and whistled through our thumbs at one another. Then all the single young men in the settlement (John and Hugh Miller, Oakley Flanigan, Willie Bishop, Norman Rowan, Jim Miller, Roy Hagler, Elmer Hiller, Gilbert Etherton, Bill Allen, and others) got the idea of developing signals to whistle up our circle of friends. One would send out the signal, and the one on the next hill would send it along to the next until everybody got the message. Then we all got together and had a little party—pretty mild by today's standards, but we had fun nonetheless.

I do have to admit that the young people of Makanda had their problems. Liquor was voted out; the livery stable went broke; and there were only two horses in town, and they belonged to the doctor. There were just two ways to get out of town: walk, or ride the train. Since money was rather scarce and hard to come by, the young men didn't ride the trains very much—that is, as paying passengers. Instead, they became quite expert at hopping freights. At least they thought they were expert, until they began having accidents. Three of them—Charley Wiley, Fred Halstead, and Willie Harris—each got a foot cut off. Two others each lost a hand, and one was killed. A girl was also killed. No, of course she wasn't hopping a freight; the fast mail got her at the crossing. She was John Wiseman's daughter.

A safer and more conventional pastime had some avid followers, both young and old, in Makanda. This was a baseball town. The ballpark was just north of the old freight house, between the railroad and the highway on the east side of town. Makanda had a team, and a good one. Almost every surrounding school district also had a team, and they all wanted to play Makanda. When I was about eighteen years old and living in the Rock Springs School District in Makanda Township, our team got its chance. The game went along for eight innings about as expected— they were winning. They had us beaten by two runs, 4 to 2. In the last of the ninth inning, we had three on base, and I was up to bat. I could throw and field, but I was not a hitter. My team all ganged around me and tried to get me to let somebody bat that had some sort of a chance. But I was contrary. The more they argued, the hotter I got—it was my turn, and I meant to have it. I stepped up to the plate and looked down at the pitcher. There he stood, all squared away and ready, with a big smirk on his face. That finished me off. I was lean and strong, and I was blind with rage. I was aware that the pitcher was throwing the ball, but I had no memory later of seeing it coming. The next thing I knew, the bat met the ball—it sounded like a rifle shot. The ball went about twenty feet over second base and kept on going. It landed right in the middle of the railroad's bar pit, which was all grown up in willows and had about a foot of water in it. Everybody on both teams just stood there gawking, and nobody made a move to try to retrieve it (that ball may be out there yet). I and my teammates on first, second, and third finally came to our senses and walked around the bases. We beat them 6 to 4. The whole team

RAPID TRANSIT 1905.

MURPHYSBORO. ILL

A 1905 photograph of the Murphysboro Street Railway. The author and several other young men occasionally took the Illinois Central's passenger train from Makanda through Carbondale to Murphysboro to see ballgames played at the city park. After the games, while they were waiting for their return train, they rode the streetcar up and down the length of Walnut Street (you could ride as long as you wanted for five cents). There were two streetcars—one closed for inclement weather and one open. Doubletrees were attached to both ends of the cars. The car in use was drawn by mules along street tracks. At the east end of the railway, the mules were unhitched and the car reversed on a turntable; at the west end there was a circle track. The car seats were also reversible. The trip was slow, and to liven things up a bit the author and his friends would run the length of the car to the front, jump off, go to the back, and jump on again. Mr. Milligan, the driver, had his work cut out for him but soon resigned himself to these youthful shenanigans. This "rapid-transit" system was the forerunner to the Murphysboro and Southern Illinois Interurban cable car that ran between Murphysboro and Carbondale. After the author moved from Makanda to Murphysboro Township in 1915, he rode the cable car for necessary trips between Murphysboro and Carbondale because it was more convenient than taking the train.

gathered around me and congratulated me on winning the game, and I was feeling pretty important—for about five minutes. Then one of them said, "What's the matter with us? He never could hit a ball before, and he probably never will again." And away went my chance for fame and fortune!

But beating Makanda was serious business. We had done something we weren't supposed to do. Nobody said a word—we didn't want to fight the whole town. We began to straggle off the field across the road to get a drink of water. We passed by a group of women who had gathered to watch the game. Several of them accused us then and there of "pulling something." We didn't argue with them, and that made them crazy. We quickly retreated and went back uptown and just kept quiet. Some of the older men who were watching had gotten quite a kick out of the whole thing. Frank Hopkins and some of his friends stepped off the distance after we left—they claimed it was something over four hundred feet. Several years later, my wife went back to Makanda to visit some of her girlhood friends, and they asked her what kind of a stunt I had pulled that day. But these were *real* people. If their team had won the game, they would have kept quiet about it, just as we did. They were, very simply, locked-in and loyal to their own little world—a world they had made for themselves there in Makanda.

◈ Salad Days

3

Education, Country Style

In 1899 we were living on what was known as the Dick Ellis place out west of Makanda. We were in the Rock Springs School District just north of Buncombe. It was a small one-room school, and there weren't too many pupils. That winter a young man named Al Deck, just out of the Army, was our teacher. He was a rather rugged sort of man in his early twenties. His features and his manner did not encourage familiarity. He was very strict, and any students who questioned his authority did so at their own peril. He was quite a tobacco chewer, and since there were always plenty of broken windowpanes, he spit through these openings during "books," as we called our classroom activities. I recall one Monday morning he came to school with only one side of his face shaved—the other side had a week's growth of beard. His razor had just given up. You see, he was a bachelor. He lived alone in a cabin back in the woods, and he looked it. But he was business and he was tough—and we didn't forget it.

That winter in school there was another boy about my age who owned a bulldog called Bruce. Someone had kicked out one of the bottom panels of the schoolroom door, so Old Bruce just came and went as he pleased. He would come in and lie by the fire and then go out for a while. At noon hour he would go from one to another mooching—he got so fat he could hardly squeeze through the hole in the door. None of us, including the teacher, thought of fixing the door.

But our solemn and stern schoolmaster *was* enterprising, and he didn't take his position lightly. He intended for us to learn something that term. He found out right away that we didn't know our multiplication tables very well. He swore we would learn them if it took the entire term, and he said that whoever learned them first would get a prize. I hate to say it, but the rest of the kids in my class must not have been very smart—I won. I had never won a prize before and haven't won one since; and, for an eleven-year-old boy, this one was a real prize—the book *Robinson Crusoe*. On one flyleaf my teacher wrote, "Learn to labor and to wait," and on another he wrote, "Everything comes to those who can wait." I have never forgotten those words, and I was to find out in my life that they really are true. Reading this book gave me a new appetite. I began to read everything I could get my hands on, from the classics to ten-cent paperback novels. Books weren't easy to come by in those days—sometimes they were passed around from family to family. I recall with particular pleasure the winter my father read to us in the evenings from a history of the early West. I remember every detail of a picture in the book of a buckskin-clad hunter with his knife poised to make the kill as his dogs circled the hunted.

Being able to read was not a common thing then. And those who could read sometimes had, as listeners, adults and children from all around the community. Can you imagine now the whole new world this opened up for middle-aged men and women who had never had the opportunity to learn to read? Dad was a self-educated man—he only went through the third grade in school—but he was a good reader.

I recall that I once had the chance to become a teacher. Jim Youngkin was the teacher at Rock Springs when I was about eighteen years old and living on the Sager place. He was going to Carbondale to take his examination to renew his certificate to teach and tried to persuade me to go with him and take the exam for a "second-grade" certificate. If you passed that exam, you could teach elementary school. But I didn't want to be a schoolteacher.

Saline County Fever

After we had been on the Ellis farm for about a year, Dad got what we called Saline County fever. Several families from Saline County had moved to Jackson County, and they all contracted this disease at more or less frequent intervals. Well, Dad got it bad this time. You may recall that he had sold his twenty-acre farm in Saline County only about three years earlier. Now he bought twenty acres from Ed Dodd right across the drainage ditch from the place he had sold. We got the same Mr. Cox to come and move us back in his covered wagon. This was sometime in August 1900.

Saline County was *home* to Dad. Family and community ties were very close there. Get-togethers were the custom, and you would be surprised how much fun we had. Several particularly interesting gatherings took place shortly after we moved back to the Ed Dodd place. Uncle John Caraway, who lived nearby, had an organ in his home. The church organist, a young lady of a rather prominent family in the community, would come to Uncle John's to play; and others in the settlement, including an unsuccessful suitor of hers, would come to sing the old love songs. Some of these old songs were very emotional, and everyone there watched carefully to see what effect they were having on the young lady and her suitor. Courtship was a very serious business in those days. I was only eleven at the time but old enough to feel the full impact of this real-life drama.

Settling In

So we were back in Saline County and, as I said, just across the ditch from the place where we'd been living when Dad decided to emigrate to Jackson County. Of course, it took a while to get settled in a new home. Most of the land was in corn that year, and Dad got part of it in the deal. He then proceeded to get a start of livestock.

But the first thing was to get a start of chickens. One night we all walked across the fields to a neighbor's place to get a dozen hens and a rooster, for which Dad paid three dollars. No one said anything about weighing these chickens. Three dollars a dozen for hens—good laying hens, and they would throw in the rooster—was a reasonable price. How well I remember that night. You see, the reason we all went along was to carry the chickens home (a distance of something like one and one-half miles) in our hands. For the benefit of those who don't know how you go about carrying a bunch of grown chickens across country in your hands, I'll try to explain. First, the men went in with their lantern to catch the chickens; then, as they were caught, they were handed out to the women and children. We were to hold the ones handed us until the chickens were caught and paid for—a transaction that might take quite a while.

So there we stood, holding a five- or six-pound hen in each hand, waiting for the men to finish this not insignificant transfer of property. Meanwhile, these half-wild creatures were not taking the proceedings calmly. In fact, they seemed to very much resent being caught and held, and every few minutes they would go into a do-or-die effort to free themselves. These were no ordinary chickens as we know them today. It was said by some that they had crossed with the great horned owl of that region. Be that as it may, they never ceased their frantic efforts to escape, so we had to constantly maintain a very firm grip on their legs. Can you imagine how our hands and arms ached after about a half hour of this!

And then we started our trip home. As we went on our way, the chickens' determination to escape seemed to grow, and every so often some of these creatures would renew their fantastic efforts to free themselves with a great flapping of wings and blood-curdling squawks that could be heard for miles. Sometimes, if we felt our grip failing, we put them on the ground and sort of laid across them until we rested a bit and they calmed down. So, in this way, we finally got them home. When it was time to turn them loose in their coop, I found I could scarcely release my grip, and my arms felt as if they had practically been wrenched from their sockets. I will never forget that night!

Resettling

The Ed Dodd place was in the same school district as our previous Saline County home, so we went back to Shiloh School again. Everything went along fine for two or three months. Then we noticed that Dad was getting restless again. We suspected what was coming up, and sure enough, just before Christmas he walked in and said he was going to write John Wiley's widow (Mr. Wiley had died some time back). He wrote and got a reply right away—she said she needed someone to take charge of the farm and that the job was his if he wanted it. And the main house on the farm was empty. So that was it! Dad got busy at once and sold off all the things we had so painfully gathered up.It seems his desire for a steady, paying job won out over his Saline County fever.

The day after Christmas we were on our way back to the John Wiley farm in Jackson County. It was cold, so we traveled by train this time. We loaded our household goods and a very frightened little dog aboard the baggage car (he made the trip safely, but he was shaking like a leaf when we retrieved him). After we had squared things around a bit, Dad found out that he was supposed to sign a ten-year contract. Well, that almost scared him to death—he seldom stayed in one place more than a year and sometimes not that long. But he did manage to stay at the Wiley Farm *almost* a year.

Extracurricular Activities at Buncombe

After New Year's we started going to Buncombe School. We had gone there before, so it wasn't strange to us. We knew many of the pupils who attended Buncombe, but not all by any means. This was a big country school for that time, with two large rooms and, of course, two teachers. Some years there would be over one hundred pupils enrolled, and believe me, those teachers earned their pay (about twenty-five dollars per month). Quite a number of the pupils were fifteen to eighteen years old, and at that time there were six young men who must have been in their twenties. They were full-grown men with beards. The ones who were courting one or more of the older girls did shave every week or two. But some of the others who hadn't become involved in that sort of thing might not shave all winter. They grew beards like General Ulysses S. Grant's.

Of course, all kinds of problems came up at schools like Buncombe. All those grown-up girls and young men thrown together all winter—well,

Union Station in Eldorado, Illinois, where the author and his family loaded their household goods on the baggage car and set out by train for Makanda in December 1900.

things did happen, believe me. Especially when two or more of the boys decided to go for the same girl, or the other way around. But I have to admit it was mostly the boys that had the fights—and they did fight! This usually took place outside. The two young gladiators, after gathering up all the supporters each of them could muster, would quietly go around behind the coal house and proceed to settle things. I don't recall that the girl was consulted in this matter at all. The noise of battle brought others to see what was going on, and of course some little sneak would run and tell the teacher. That broke up the fight. You see, these teachers were supposed to be able to whip any pupil, no matter how old or how big. Here and now, I want to put in a plug for those schoolteachers—I never, in my fourteen terms in these country schools, saw one of them fail to do just that. At Shiloh, Rock Springs, and Buncombe I saw these battles rage, and not once did I see the teacher lose.

But there was one fight at Buncombe that did look favorable for about the first two rounds. You see, this young man was about the same age as the teacher and quite a bit bigger. He was twenty-one or twenty-two years old and, as we learned later, was to marry one of the pupils as soon as school was out in the spring. It looked as if he was trying to impress his girl—if that *was* his idea, he certainly did louse things up. But he had his campaign strategy all mapped out. One day during books a farmer came by the schoolhouse with his team and wagon, and this big shot got up from his desk and stood by the window watching him pass. The teacher told him to take his seat, but he didn't move. The teacher told him again, more firmly this time, and the young man spoke right up and said that maybe the teacher would like to come and make him take his seat. Well, there it was—a challenge that no schoolteacher could ignore. He didn't hesitate a moment but went right over to where the pupil was waiting for him. When the teacher got within reach, the pupil let go with a terrific blow that landed squarely on the teacher's chest. The force of the blow stopped him, and the rest of us thought for one glorious and never-to-be-forgotten moment that we were about to see the impossible happen right before our eyes. But it was not to be. This teacher had been and still was quite an athlete and had been in tight spots before. One terrible blow laid the pupil out cold, flat on his back, where the teacher proceeded to work him over but good. I saw this man much later when we were both growing old, and his nose was still flat. But despite his setback, he did marry the girl in the spring.

Love at First Sight

I was about the proper age and a rather husky boy, so I applied for and got the janitorial job at the school. This was quite a distinction, because the position was sought after by several boys who were about my age. It wasn't just the money (I received one dollar per month for the work); considerable prestige also went with the job. The janitor stayed after school to sweep out the entire building and was to be back by eight o'clock the next morning to dust off the seats and the teacher's desk and chair. During the day he carried in the coal, kept the fire going, and brought water from the well about one hundred yards away. Of course, he was to have the fires going in both rooms in the morning so the building would be reasonably warm when the others arrived.

One morning, after having finished my work at school, I was standing out front watching the other kids come up the path to the landing where I was. There were several steps leading up to the landing, which led into the cloakroom and then to the classroom. Then I saw this rather frail-looking little girl coming up the path. It was slightly uphill and somewhat muddy. She seemed to be having quite a struggle of it. For some reason—I didn't know why—I continued to watch her, and I forgot about the others. When she reached the steps, she took hold of the railing

The author as a boy of fourteen.

The beautiful little girl who caught the author's early attention was Bessie Mae Rowan, daughter of McFarland and Johanna Kelley Rowan. Bessie is pictured above at three years of age.

and paused for just a moment as if to catch her breath. She looked up, and we saw each other for the first time. She was wearing some sort of knitted hood—it was blue, tied with a blue ribbon. She had bright red curls and wonderful big, blue eyes that only the heavens could match. I was just a boy of twelve, but I knew even then that I had met *the* girl in my life. Her name was Bessie Mae Rowan.

Bessie Mae Rowan as a young lady of sixteen. The author first approached her at a box supper, offering her a candy heart with the inscribed message, "I love you." She tied it in the corner of her handkerchief and tucked the hanky in her waistband. She and Charless were married a few months before her eighteenth birthday.

The author as a young man of nineteen. He was twenty-one when he and Bessie were married.

About seven years later, when she was a young woman and I was a young man, I went calling on her—and that was it! But it took me almost two years to persuade her that I was the one she should marry. Why did it take so long? Well, as you might well guess, I had some very formidable and determined rivals. Some of them owned as much as 120 acres of land, with houses and everything; while I, poor boy that I was, didn't even have a place to live. But for some reason she married *me*—I was never able to figure that one out, but marry me she did at the Baptist Parsonage in Makanda on February 23, 1910.

So that was that, and we set sail on the sea of matrimony. Some folks thought it was going to be more like going over Niagara Falls in a barrel than like a launching, but we were not disturbed by their doubts. We were wearing those rose-colored glasses one hears so much about. To us, our ship of dreams was a wonderful vessel, big and seaworthy, with a spread of sail that took one's breath away. In short, this little old world was our oyster—all we had to do now was to find out how to crack the thing with nothing but our bare hands. So away we went, under full sail, with never a doubt in our minds as to what the outcome would be. It surely was a good thing we couldn't see the storm clouds that were gathering just beyond the horizon.

Love at First Sight

◆ New Ventures   4

Changing Partners

Dad had not forsaken his lifelong habit of compulsive land dealing. From my twelfth to my eighteenth year, we had moved from the main house on the John Wiley farm (where we lived after our second trek to Jackson County) to the tenant house there, to the Ben Wiley farm, back to the tenant house on the John Wiley farm, to the Al McMurphy farm, to the McKinnon farm, and to the George Hiller place, as it was called. In Jackson County Dad always rented or hired out his services, knowing that he would eventually go back to Saline County. Except for temporary places of residence, he always owned his homes in Saline County. In fact, he held the record at Harrisburg, the county seat, for real estate transactions.

When my wife and I were first married, we lived with Mother and Dad on the George Hiller place. My two sisters, Emma and Ella, had already married and were living in Carbondale. The Hiller place lay just south of what is now Midland Hills Lake—in fact, about half the lake is on this farm. At the time we lived there, of course, the lake had not been built. Frank Krysher owned the Hiller place, and it was he who put over the idea of building a lake there. Later, when we were living on the Sager place east of there where the Midland Hills golf course now lies, I, with some others, cleared the valley for the lake.

Dad and I farmed the Hiller place as partners—he kept the chores up, and I did the team work. The first crop we made there in 1906 was a

Emma (left) and Ella as young women. They married brothers—Frank and Arthur Hiller. Three of the author's sisters—Betty, Nellie, and a twin to Emma—died as infants.

good one. Corn and sweet potatoes were the main crops. The corn was mostly for feed, although we did sell some white corn to Frank Sumner, who ran the mill at Makanda. Some years we got one dollar per bushel for this milling corn. The potatoes were sold to Curt Hagler, who bought all the sweet potatoes grown in that vicinity. He owned three big storage houses—one on his home place, one in Boskeydell (a small community a few miles north of Makanda), and one in Makanda—and had a part interest in one at Etherton Switch (a village a few miles south of Murphysboro). The potatoes were kept in storage until sometime in the winter, when prices were about as high as they were likely to get.

In the winter of 1910–11, after the crops were in, Dad began to get restless again. Along towards spring he and Mother moved out. Their new place south of Murphysboro in Cedar Bottoms was owned by a Carbondale real estate man named Boos. They lived in the "House on the

Rose Oldenhage (left) and Emma Caraway Hiller in a picture taken in 1912. This rather elegant means of transportation was typical of the times.

Bluff," as it was called, rent free; were furnished a horse and wagon for their transportation; and received twenty dollars a month just to look after the place. Dad said he had been thinking of quitting farming anyway, and he thought that this would be a good time—my wife and I were expecting a baby in the summer.

The author's parents, Merritt M. and Melvina Powell Caraway, shown here at ages 68 and 64, respectively. After leaving the George Hiller place in Makanda Township, they would make one more pilgrimage to Saline County together. Melvina died in Carbondale Township in Jackson County at age 66. Merritt moved back and forth several times but returned to Jackson County to stay when he was 75. He died in Carbondale Township at age 87.

A Family of Our Own

On June 10, 1911, our firstborn arrived, right in the middle of crop season. Lester was a big, fine boy, and he got along well. But his mother didn't do so well—she developed what the doctor called rheumatism in her leg, and she was in bed for six weeks. I kept fairly busy waiting on them, doing the cooking and washing, and finishing with the crop. Of

Merritt and Melvina on the porch of their little rose-covered cottage in Eldorado—the last home they were to share together there.

course, I only worked eight-hour shifts . . . anywhere from two to three of them every twenty-four hours.

While my patients were still bedfast, a terrible storm came up. I was holding the dining room door, or trying to, when the force of the wind became so strong that it took the door right off the hinges and slammed it back on top of the dining table. It sure didn't do the dishes any good! I quickly retreated to the room where Bessie and the baby were and managed to hold that door until the storm passed.

Our second son, George, was born in August the following year. He also was a fine, healthy boy, and there was no trouble this time. We

George, a friend (Edward Stotlar), and Lester when the family lived on the Waller place.

were quite thrilled that we had two boys "right off the reel," as the saying goes. Now we were a real family—Mom and Dad and Lester and George.

Burned Out

Everything went along just fine for us until early in November the next year, 1913, when the house caught fire and burned to the ground with practically everything we had in the way of food, clothing, and household goods. With winter coming on, it did bring up some problems. But as the old minister said (when on his way home from church the lady just in front of him lost her leghorn hat in the breeze and its landed squarely in his arms), "The Lord will provide." George Hiller still owned the adjoining farm, and he and his wife had just moved to Carbondale. He let us live in his vacant home on the Old Jonesboro Road (now U.S. Route 51) until we could find a place. With the help of our neighbors, we got through until spring.

Party Line

When my wife and I moved into the George Hiller home near Makanda, we had a telephone for the first time. They were just coming into general use, and I do mean use. One lady reportedly spent so much time listening in on the party line that she had a permanent indentation in her chin from leaning on the mouthpiece. Uncle Will Rowan of Makanda had both a telephone and a "talking machine." He was really proud of that phonograph. Once in a while, when someone would call him up, he would put it by the telephone and play one of his favorite records, "The Wreck of Old Ninety-Seven," for everyone on the line.

Roughing It

We still had the George Hiller farm rented from Frank Krysher, but no house. Then Lon Hiller (George Hiller's brother) let us move into a cabin on his place, which joined the Krysher farm. We lived there the summer of 1914. This cabin was about one-quarter of a mile across Pisque Hollow from the place where I made my crop and cared for the livestock. I traveled back and forth as I went about my work.

I had gathered up a bunch of hogs, about twenty head in all. They were about the best thing going for the small farmer. I had put some money and considerable feed into this venture, and we were depending on these hogs to put us on our feet again; but providence or luck, or whatever you may call it, did not cooperate. Hog cholera swept through the countryside. It left us with only three hogs—barely enough for our meat, and we were thankful for that.

There was one thing that I had needed very much to get along with the farming—a good, young team of mules to work. As it was out of the question to buy them, I had decided to get a brood mare and raise them myself. I proceeded to do just that. The first spring (after our house had burned in the fall) the mare brought a fine mule colt. Well, *maybe* you can imagine how proud I was of this very fine colt—I doubt it, though.

While we were living in our temporary cabin home, which was primitive with a dirt floor and cracks in the walls, I bought a fresh side of bacon. Now just down the valley a way was a very rugged piece of land with great bluffs and hills. It was cutover land with quite a few bobcats. Of course, they weren't dangerous—but try telling that to a woman and two small children after a bobcat had tried to get at their meat supply by digging under the cabin wall. The evening that happened, I was coming home from my day's work, and it wasn't quite dark yet. I heard something coming through the brush, and it was stirring up quite a ruckus. I stopped to watch as it came along the hillside, some hundred or so feet away. I could see the bulk of him—that was about all—but I knew by the way he got over the ground that this was something one didn't see every day. When I reached the cabin and my wife finally opened the door, she was standing there holding a worn-out butcher knife in her hand. No, I wouldn't say that she was scared—I never saw her actually scared in my life. The boys were in bed all covered up, and she was going to fight that varmint with whatever weapon there was at hand. If the shotgun that went with the cabin had been there, I am sure the bobcat population would have been minus one very brave and venturesome member. As it was, he learned one thing for sure—tunneling in is a dangerous business. What a story he must have told the gang that night! I wonder how he explained his split nose—I'll bet he didn't poke it through another crack for a while, anyway. He probably made it sound like just another event in the life of a Southern Illinois bobcat. And, I must say, if you haven't heard a couple of these varmints screaming their defiance at each other and, judging by the sound they make, at the whole world, then you have no idea of the thrills and chills that you can experience right here in Southern Illinois!

A New Start

That fall we moved on to the farm just east of the cabin. A man by the name of Charles E. Sager, who lived in Springfield, owned the place (this was the Old McKinnon farm that Dad rented when I was about sixteen and where the Midlands Hills golf course was to be built). There was a good log house, outbuildings, and 120 acres of land, such as it was. We didn't do so good that year—the summer was very dry. But we had a cow and a calf, hogs for our meat, and some chickens. There was fruit and, of course, we grew everything we could to eat. So we weren't too bad off.

All the while, I was taking the best care I could of my brood mare and her mule colt. Everything seemed to be going along all right. Then the mare brought another mule colt just like the first one. Now I *know* you can't imagine how I felt—a pair of the finest mule colts in the neighborhood, and they belonged to me! But the little colt lived just three days.

No, I didn't give up on the mule deal—not on your life. How could we give up? We were young, gloriously young—I was twenty-four and my wife was twenty—and our lives were so irrevocably joined there was no thought of turning back. So we laid our plans for the future. I traded the mule I had left for another brood mare and got fifty dollars to boot. Both mares brought mule colts the next spring. I kept these mules and broke them to work. They were a good team, and they did the plowing and hauling for twenty years. And no one except me or one of our boys ever harnessed or hitched these mules. They didn't make friends easily, if you know what I mean.

Invaded

Shortly before we moved away from the Sager place in Makanda Township in the fall of 1915, we were invaded by a nomadic "tribe" that came swarming down from the north. We were still trying to recover from being burned out late in 1913 and having to live the next summer in a sawmill cabin before we moved onto the Sager place in the fall of 1914. We had no warning of any kind; it was really a bolt right out of the blue. There were only eleven in the tribe, but they made up in other ways for what they lacked in numbers.

It was a hot, dry August. I was working for Frank Krysher, clearing the brush so he could sow the land down in grass. Wages had gone up quite a bit by then—we were getting ten cents an hour. So, if you could stand that kind of work for ten hours, you had earned a token good for one dollar's worth of groceries at the store in Makanda. I had just completed one of these ten-hour shifts on the hillside and walked three-quarters of a mile home. As I came up to the house, I saw a man sitting there by himself, smoking a cigarette. By the number of butts lying around, I guessed he had been holding down that seat on the cistern curb for some time. I am sure that for a full minute we just looked at each other. I was in no mood for talking, and it seemed he was having trouble getting started. So I decided to give him more time to think it over. As I started to the barn to finish the chores, he caught up with me and began to tell me that he had rented the farm that joined the place where we lived and that he and his family should stay with us until their things arrived by train and they could get moved in. It seemed as though the man who owned the farm he rented had "recommended" us. I hadn't said anything up to this point; in fact, I'm not at all sure that I could have spoken if I had tried. Everyone had forgotten to let *us* know what *they* had decided we should do.

Between the house and the barn there were several big and very old peach trees. While the man was explaining everything to me, his nine youngsters were putting on a first-class "chimp" circus, chasing each other through these trees. Were they falling and breaking their arms and their legs? Not on your life. Did you ever hear of a chimp falling out of a tree and breaking a leg? There was one caper, though, that did hold some promise for a moment or two. One chased another out on one of those big, high limbs. The strain became too great and down came limb, peaches, youngsters, and all in one heap. After I "explained" things to the tribal chief, he made me a very generous offer for the peaches.

And then it was suppertime. The women had figured out that my family would eat first and our "guests" later. The next morning we had the same arrangement. But the man was still asleep in *my* bed when *I* went to work! And the evening and the morning were the first day. And it went on something like that for the next three days. Their things finally did arrive, and we were all in our separate houses at last. I charged fifteen cents a meal for boarding them (the landlord was paying their bills).

We were ready to make a move ourselves. In September 1915 we moved to the Modglin farm near Etherton Switch. About a year later my parents moved to the Elmer Hiller farm nearby. As soon as I knew about their move, I went over to see them. Dad was working a short distance from the road, and I went out to meet him. I had been there just a few minutes when a man stopped his team and jumped out of the wagon and came running toward us. He threw his arms around me, and I would almost swear there were tears in his eyes. I didn't recognize my former guest—he had grown a full beard. He began telling Dad (he didn't know he was talking to my father) what a fine man I was and went on to tell how I, out of the goodness of my heart, had taken his family in and kept them until they could get located. Then he patted me on the back and hugged me some more. He seemed to be a very emotional man, and so was Dad. Then the man found out who Dad was, and they started hugging each other and me by turns. I had never been in a fix like that before, and I became flustered. So what was I doing? Mostly just standing there looking at the toes of my shoes, and learning how a fairly respectable dog feels while the sheep wool is plucked from between his teeth.

Well, it finally ended, and the man went on his way. I got on my horse and headed for home. The horse had an easy trip—I was in no hurry. I had some thinking to do, and I had a strange feeling that maybe I wouldn't be coming out of this thing lily white. "Out of the goodness of his heart." That's what the man said.

Invaded

◈ Blessings and Burdens 5

Greener Pastures

By the summer of 1915, it seemed to us that we had just about skimmed the cream off Makanda Township, so we decided it was time to seek greener pastures. Luck was on our side again. One of our neighbors told us of a farm for rent in the township to the north and west. As I've mentioned, this was the Modglin farm near Etherton Switch in Murphysboro Township. It was only eight or ten miles away, but it might as well have been a hundred. We had heard of the place, sure. We had heard of Little Rock, Arkansas, too. And just about as much of one as the other. But we made a deal for this farm for one year. We barely knew the man we dealt with, and we had never heard of the owner, his brother, who was living in Florida. The owner and his brother had to sue the man who lived on the farm to get him to vacate the premises. They finally got him out, and we moved in. The move wasn't as simple as it might sound. Of course, everything was done with teams at that time. I got one of my neighbors to help me on the trip, and with the two wagons we took enough of our household goods and the chickens so my wife and the boys could stay at the new place while I went back after the rest of our things. One trip a day was all I could make up and down those hills and across those creeks. But we finally made it!

We were living in a foreign land, and the natives, by one means or another, saw to it that we didn't forget that fact. Please don't misunderstand. These were honest, hard-working farm people, and I'm sure they meant no harm to anyone. They were all related by blood or marriage;

From the early 1890s to about 1918, the Carbondale Opera House occupied the top floors of this building (the original home of the First National Bank of Carbondale) at Main and Washington streets. Late in the summer of 1915, the author was called to Carbondale as a witness in the litigation concerning his rental of the Ott Modglin farm near Etherton Switch. Frank Krysher, his former landlord and friend (and Carbondale mayor from 1919 to 1922) also attended the proceedings. That evening the author had a once-in-a-lifetime treat. Krysher took him to the opera house, where they saw a live performance of *The Virginian*. This historic building has come full circle: it is now the home of a community theater group called The Stage Company. The author's grandniece, Joanne Parrish Cross, is a member of the group.

they were all landowners by inheritance; and they just could barely tolerate, much less understand, this family of "gypsies" being dumped right into the midst of their close-knit community. But there we were, and there we stayed.

We rented in Murphysboro Township for about eight years—we moved from the Modglin farm to the Mike Ira place, to the Ed Waller place, back to the Mike Ira place, and to the Charlie Blust place—and we did fairly well for sharecroppers. We had saved a little money. Our neighbors were watching and waiting. So one day I had a caller, and he happened to have one of the largest landholdings in the community. He had sold a part of his farm, for a considerable down payment and with the balance to be paid so much each year, to a man who had failed to meet the payments. So the owner got the land back, and now he was looking for another "fish." He figured we had a little money, and he had done quite a bit of talking about selling this piece of land to us "peasants." His plan was to collect the down payment and interest again and then get the land back. I took the "bait," and in 1924, only three years later, we had paid for the place. Since we had five years to pay the balance, he was the one who was left open-mouthed and gasping for air. To say he was flabbergasted would be putting it mildly, much too mildly. I think the word discombobulated would be better. The impossible had happened. Who did these upstarts from way down there in the hills south of Cedar Creek think they were, anyway, to buy this land and actually pay for it? He had been robbed of two years of interest! But he was a man after my own heart. I never had a better neighbor. In a business deal he asked no quarter and gave none, and that suited me fine. We had clawed our way up this far, and there was no place for sentiment in our business dealings! This man, Lewis Etherton, and his most gracious wife became our best friends. When they came around to our side, they came the full circle. They had seen us become landowners by our *own* efforts—now, they thought we could do just about anything.

It has been fifty years now since we moved to Murphysboro Township, and in all those years we have never lived more than one mile from the Modglin farm, the first place we rented there. For the past forty years we have owned the land that joined that place on the north. We didn't make the move to Murphysboro Township to improve our social position—we had to make a living for our family, and that was about it.

When I was still a small boy, I was very aware of a built-in desire to own a piece of land some day. When I married, my wife and I set a time and savings schedule for ourselves. It had taken fifteen years of renting and sacrificing, but we made our goal, almost to the year. We finally had our home place. The need to feed hungry mouths is a powerful incentive, but we were driven by another force, too—a love of the land. Our land.

Invaded Again

This time the invasion came from the south. We were still living on the Modglin place near Etherton Switch. It was the Fourth of July, 1916, and the city of Murphysboro was having a big celebration. But we had to stay home and look after our chickens and things. So we went about the task of gathering and preparing the makings of a big, country-style, feed— fried chicken, new potatoes, green beans, roasting ears, and the trimmings. The day wore on and grew hotter and hotter. By the time we had eaten our dinner, all we could do was make a pallet in the living room and lie down and take it easy. We roused up about the middle of the afternoon and saw that it was looking like rain. About five o'clock we finished off what was left of the food, and it was a good thing we did. We didn't get much to eat for the next thirty-six hours!

About that time the storm clouds began to appear in the northwest. We knew that three wagonloads of our friends and neighbors (one family with parents, children, in-laws, and all—about thirty of them) were in Murphysboro celebrating. They all lived south of Cedar Creek, and we began to think what a mess they would be in if Cedar Bottoms overflowed. The clouds came on fast, and soon the rain was pouring down. We congratulated ourselves for staying home and pitied those people who would be caught in all that rain.

A short time later I went to the door to see how everything was doing, and the three wagons were just pulling into our barn lot. The barn had a large entryway, so they parked the wagons in there. The women and children began getting out and making a run for our house. We just stood there sort of stunned as if we couldn't believe what we were seeing. Of course, we did the best we could for them. The living room was small, and they just about filled it up. They took turns going in to the kitchen to wring out their clothes. That was about all they could do.

The next thing was to prepare somehow for the night. We spread down such as we had in the way of quilts and anything else we could find. And so we bedded down a whole room full (just about as close as they could lie) of wet people. And it was a very hot night. We slept in our beds, or tried to—as you may have guessed, the situation was not conducive to a good night's sleep!

The women were up early the next morning preparing breakfast, which consisted mostly of fried potatoes, gravy, biscuits, and coffee. The feeding process went on without a break until about four in the after-

A 1928 photograph of one of the fine old homes in the village of Etherton Switch. Several members of the Sherwood family are pictured here. At one time there were twelve homes in this flourishing valley community about six miles south of Murphysboro. The village was named after the Etherton family, which owned land along Sugar Creek where the railroad switch was built. A two-story brick general store, where the author often went for supplies, was the hub of activity during Etherton's heyday (1900–1930), with a post office, the Woodmen of the World lodge hall upstairs, and a large front porch where the men of the village—mostly farmers and railroad section hands—gathered to talk after trading. Several area men cut railroad ties up on Hickory Ridge and traded them in at the store; when enough ties were collected, the railroad picked them up. One of the inducements to this trading was fresh bread dropped in large boxes from the train several times a week. Etherton also boasted a garage/blacksmith shop on the south side of the store, the famous sweet-potato storage house (a two-story heated wood building with a basement), a flour mill, a church, a packing shed where area fruit was processed for shipment by truck and rail, and a village well.

noon. As the day wore on, the coffee grew weaker and weaker, the biscuits grew soggier (the grease was running low), and the potatoes were so small the peelers could scarcely keep up with the fryers. A riot almost broke out when one of the girls "traded" plates with her sister when she wasn't looking. I couldn't say for sure that the shortage of supplies influenced our visitors' decision to try to get back on the other side of Cedar Creek, but I suspect it did. Luckily, they did make it back home.

I had told my wife that as soon as they were gone I would go to Etherton Switch and get some food, since there was very little left and no time to go to Murphysboro with the team and wagon. But when I got to the village, I discovered that the storekeeper, Henry Sauer, was in the process of closing out his entire stock—he was about to sell and, of course, hadn't ordered any new supplies. So there we were holding the short end of the stick again, and there wasn't a thing we could do about it. Yes, we had supper—little cull potatoes, with no bread since we had no lard.

But I liked the leader of this group of invaders. He was down-to-earth with a way about him that appealed to me. And if the circumstances had been reversed, he would have shared his home with me and my family as long as was necessary and never said a word.

A Gypsy Caravan

In the early 1900s the Old Jonesboro Road south from Carbondale in Jackson County was a main gypsy trail. Another trail (now Illinois Route 127) led south from Murphysboro. I had lived most of my life in between these two roads and had seen a lot of gypsies.

One particularly interesting group appeared when we lived on the Modglin place east of Etherton Switch in 1917. Part of this place ran down by the road the gypsies traveled. There was a little creek nearby with plenty of water and grassy banks, and the caravan picked this spot for their campsite. They came to our house at the top of the hill to get permission to camp there. They were a kind of traveling circus. They had in all about thirty-five head of horses (most of them trading stock), several ponies (a few of these had an extra foot on each of their front legs), two large brown bears that performed, a bucking mule, and an "educated" horse. Theirs was a business proposition. Everywhere they stopped, they set up a show. This one was inside what I used for my pasture, and their wagons were parked just outside my fence. The gypsies sold tickets and had a wagonload of folding chairs to seat their customers. Of course, we didn't have to pay to get in, but everybody else did.

A prize was offered to anybody who would wrestle one of the bears and stay with him two minutes. Pete Mathis, the section foreman on the Gulf, Mobile & Ohio Railroad which ran through Etherton Switch, took on the job. The bear lost his muzzle during the scuffle, and it seemed for a minute that he might bite Pete's arm off. It scared everyone nearly to death, including the gypsies! They corralled the bear and took him back outside the fence to the wagon. The other bear had gotten out of his cage and was also loose. That created quite a commotion, but the gypsies finally got them both back in the wagon. Then they offered a prize to anyone who would ride the bucking mule. No one volunteered, so one of their own men undertook this feat. He maneuvered around until they were up on the hillside and then kicked the mule in the ribs. The mule turned his tail end straight up and threw the man about twenty feet down the hillside, where he landed right on his nose. That was enough of that! So they brought out the educated horse. They fed him a little information—the year and the month you were born—and the horse would tell you what day of the month your birthday fell on by picking up wooden blocks and laying them aside in the proper order. They would ask the horse something and he would nod his head up and down or sideways to indicate whether or not he understood. And that was the show.

The next day the gypsies began to spread out over the countryside in teams of three or four. While the men got your attention, the women, dressed in Mother Hubbards, would forage for eggs in the chicken houses and barns and for whatever else they could find in the gardens and fields. It was quite an experience. The natives soon caught on and the gypsies went on their way, pasturing off the roadside and "living off the land," so to speak. Etherton Switch seemed like a powerfully dull place after that—particularly to our two sons, who were five and six years old at the time.

A Gypsy Caravan

◆

Unfortunately . . .

We had moved to the Modglin farm in September 1915. War was threatening to engulf the world, and eventually America joined forces with its allies abroad to aid them in the struggle. In the spring of 1917, when I was twenty-eight, the first draft call was issued for men from twenty-one to thirty years old. I was the 211th man called to Murphysboro for a physical examination. I was classified 1A. Farmers like myself were given thirty days to make necessary business and family arrangements when they were called into service. I didn't think too much about my situation because all the other men in my age group in the community had been called for examinations also. But my wife was worried about what would happen to her and our two young sons. Then President Woodrow Wilson, who was a saving man, made the decision that he would fight the war with single men (we assumed his reason was to avoid support payments to the families of married men). I was reclassified, as were others in my position.

Considerable sacrifice was made at home, and stringent laws were passed concerning the production and use of foodstuffs so there would be plenty to send overseas. You couldn't even have a chicken dinner without breaking the law; chickens were for laying eggs. There were very few chiselers. No self-respecting citizen would have even thought of violating the law in the national emergency. But the truth is Wilson's food administrator, Herbert Hoover, very nearly starved us all to death. And stories came back to us of the terrible waste of precious food sent to Europe. Then the enemy was defeated as support fell away. In November 1918, two days after the fighting had ceased, our neighbor, Lon Hagler, who had a telephone, came to our house—we had moved to the Mike Ira place early that year—to tell us that the war was over.

After the war, the American farmer continued his extra effort to feed a devastated and hungry Europe. Hoover, one of the greatest civil engineers the world will ever see, administered this program also. And then, unfortunately, he managed to get himself elected president!

Luckier than Some

And so one agony was over. But swiftly on its heels came a deadly influenza epidemic. This great epidemic, which killed an estimated twenty million people worldwide and over five hundred thousand Americans, made it way to Murphysboro Township. Our youngest son, George, woke up in the middle of the night delirious with fever. Then Lester came down. And then my wife. I managed to look after the livestock, keep the fires in the stove going, and make chicken soup for my three patients. Then, of course, I caught it, too. But I couldn't go to bed because I had to take care of the others.

People all around were dying. Sometimes entire families. Old people and children seemed to go first. And men, trying to keep up with their chores after they took sick, developed pneumonia and died. Most of these people had never been to a doctor in their lives. They did the best they could to take care of their own.

We were luckier than some of our neighbors. It really knocked us for a loop, but we all lived. It was nearly a year, though, before I was back to normal. In the spring when I started to break the ground for planting, my legs were so weak they would hardly hold me and my knees ached almost unbearably. But gradually I got better. I had to. That was the only way I could make a living.

We would escape another catastrophic event some time later. After the purchase of our home place in 1924 from Lewis Etherton, we settled in for the winter. The following March the city of Murphysboro and surrounding areas were devastated by a tornado. In Murphysboro alone, over two hundred people were killed, eight hundred were injured, and eight thousand were left homeless. This tornado, which swept through Missouri, Illinois, and Indiana, was one of the worst American disasters ever. Our place was about five miles off its path, but even at that distance the suction force of the wind caused the windowpanes in the house to bow out. We didn't know the extent of the storm until Lester and

George came home from school with the news that Murphysboro had been "blown away."

Hanging On

Blessings and Burdens

In the early 1900s the government was not helping the poor. We had some very conservative administrations led by men like Taft, Harding, Coolidge, and last but not least, Mr. Hoover—the only man who, in his own words, ever had a depression named after him. We had just paid off the mortgage on the farm we purchased and barely had time to heave a great sigh of relief when, lo and behold, the bottom fell out of the stock market. In fact, the bottom fell out of everything. Good hogs were selling for only three cents or less per pound, and shipping expenses didn't come down. Other farm products were hit just as hard. After a few years of this—just barely hanging on by our eyebrows—we were the nearest to being whipped we had ever been. I think it was about this time that Hoover immortalized himself by making a great speech in which he told us we could lick the depression if we would all save our money. Oh, yes, it sounded fine. There was just one thing wrong—very few people had any money to save. But we had a "foothold on a hillside," and it was going to take more than a little old ten-year depression to dislodge us. The going got pretty rough, but we made it!

◆ Harvest Years

6

A Land-Hungry Tribe

Our two older boys were growing up, and our family had increased by three: another son, Wayne, and two daughters, Ethel and Cleo. So we had to plan bigger and work harder. Some old-timers in the community had passed on, and some had quit farming—their land had been depleted to the point where they figured it was better just to let it lie. We rented some of this land for corn, stock peas, and other hay crops. The yield was small, but we were used to that and we were thankful for any little thing we got. We were a tribe now, and a land-hungry tribe. And lying all about us was this apparently unwanted and unused land—several hundred acres of it. Very few people were in the market for tracts of worn-out land. It would sell cheaply one of these days, and we went about the business of being ready for that day.

And time marched on. (I can't say that I particularly admire the setup, but that seems to be the way it works!) The older boys were grown men, and we had two more children—Charley and Betty. We had managed, just barely, to survive the Great Depression, and times were getting better. We had a president who could see and hear; he also had a brain and, best of all, a heart. So the pieces began to fall in place.

Lewis Etherton, our good friend and neighbor from whom we had bought our first piece of land, had passed on, as had the landowner with the next largest tract. Their farms joined, and their land joined ours. There it was—this worn-out but still (to us) beautiful farmland with fields

Three-year-old Wayne in the yard of the Blust place, where the family lived for a while. The empty chair was for baby sister Ethel, who declined to be photographed.

of up to sixty acres suitable for power farming. It almost seemed that people knew when we had saved enough to buy a parcel of this land.

Our eldest son, Lester, bought an eighty that cornered our place and later bought two additional forties that fronted on the main highway (Route 127). Around this time our three younger sons—George, Wayne, and Charley—were serving overseas in World War II. When I heard about the pending sale of Lewis Etherton's home place, I wrote to George in England to alert him. He had to wait a while, but he did buy it; and, as time went by, he bought other land that joined his. Charley bought a tract just across the highway. And my wife and I added another forty to our farm.

After about twenty years of this sort of thing, our holdings now add up to just about a section (a standard section is 640 acres), not square

The family's pet billy goat with Ethel (left) and Cleo at the home place.

Camera-shy Cleo inspecting a flower in the yard at the home place where she was born.

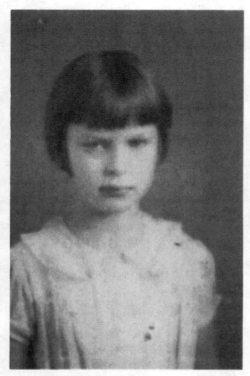

The author's two youngest children, Charley and Betty, in early grade-school pictures at Sharon School.

but pretty well bunched together. There are no debts, mortgages, or outstanding claims of any sort. And we have had no serious problems about paying our taxes. Lester and George have around 175 head of good Hereford cattle, and George raises upwards of 300 head of market hogs each year. Yields per acre of 70 or 80 bushels of corn are the usual, and 100-bushel yields have been recorded. For soybeans, a yield per acre of 25 to 40 bushels is about what one can expect. The long-abused and worn-out land is producing again.

Inspection day at Sharon School, the one-room country school (with a library and two cloak-rooms) about three miles from the author's place. All the Caraway children graduated from this school. Pictured (left to right) in the first row are Opal Hickam, Evelyn Grammer, Helen Raines, Cleo Caraway, Alma Waller, Roberta Moore, and Clarence Moore; in the second row, Ethel Caraway, Carl Raines, Jack Raines, John Morefield, Eugene Jones, and Wayne Caraway; and in the third row, Catherine Raines, Vera Jones, Esther Morefield, Mrs. Lena Doody, and Lewis "Ebb" Etherton. Mrs. Doody taught at Sharon School for four years. "Ebb" (the son of the author's neighbor, Lewis Etherton) was the Jackson County superintendent of schools from 1927 until his death in 1943. The author served on the Sharon School Board for many years.

A Puppy Tale

No, life at the home place was not all grim determination. Of course there was a lighter side . . .

This farmhouse, built in the early 1870s, was the home place of Lewis Etherton, from whom the author bought his first piece of land. George Caraway purchased this house and the surrounding 160-acre farm in 1948.

I must tell you a story about a little pup who was very unlucky—he was born the wrong color. His master decided to get rid of him for fear he would spoil the sale of the others in the litter. So one summer evening he took him up the road about two miles and left him close to the home of a family—mine—where he knew there was a bunch of kids and no dog. It was about suppertime, and maybe the pup smelled the food cooking. Anyway, he seemed to have had no trouble finding us. I was lying out on the porch, enjoying the cool of the evening. I must have dozed off. Suddenly I felt something warm and wet slap me in the face. I opened my eyes and there was this fine, big pup, about six or eight weeks old, all fat, fuzzy, and sleek, and apparently very glad to make my acquaintance. After a while we went to spread the news of his arrival, and this seemed to be just what he had been looking for. After about an hour or so of getting

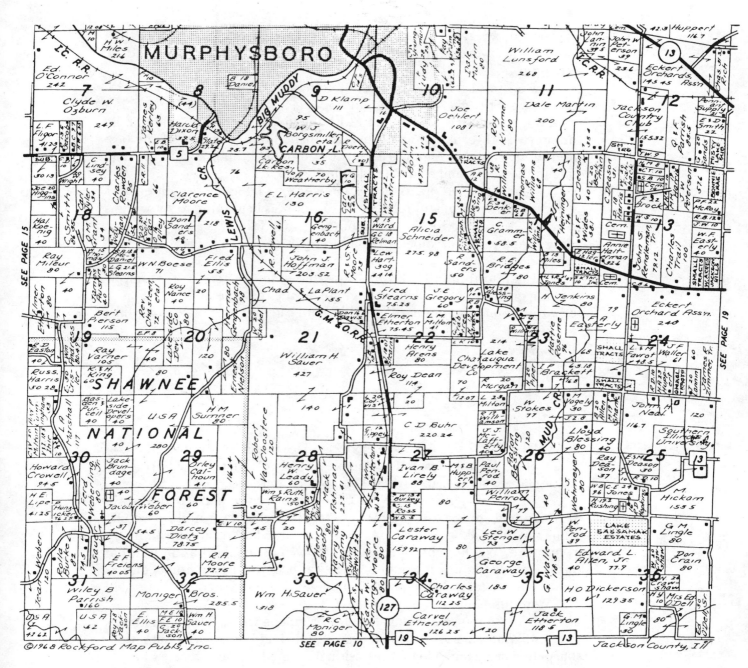

A 1968 plat map showing Caraway land ownership in sections 27, 34, and 35.

acquainted, several of the smaller kids' faces were somewhat cleaner than usual and we were all ready to call it a day. The pup had a home and we had a pup.

And so began twelve years of companionship for us and the rejected pup. Fritz grew to be a good dog. He always behaved himself as a good dog should. He would romp with the kids or fight anything that he thought was threatening any of us. He turned out to be one of the best hunting dogs in that region—a tree dog at night, a rabbit dog in the daytime in the fields, and a squirrel dog in the woods.

Time rambled on, as usual. Twelve years later the two older boys were full-grown men and I, believe it or not, was beginning to show signs of aging. According to the nature of things, Ol' Fritz was a very old dog, ailing in many ways. Something had to be done, and I was the one who had to do it.

I like to think that Fritz is out yonder somewhere in that happy hunting ground where all good dogs go, having the time of his life, romping with his buddies or chasing rabbits, and catching one once in a while.

Another Breed of Cat

You will recall my story about the bobcat that visited our cabin on the Lon Hiller place. Well, I must tell you about another cat that showed up at our home place several years after we had settled in there.

I can't imagine for the life of me how it ever happened, but we were suddenly out of cats. There wasn't a cat on the place, and we weren't doing anything about it. One day an ornery little kitten came strolling up in the yard. We thought, of course, that we had acquired a cat, but that wasn't exactly the way it would be. The cat had acquired a home, and *he* would have to tolerate the people who lived there, if he could. We called him Wampus.

Everything went along all right for quite a while. Although he was well fed, Wampus was still a small cat. But he had big feet and long, well-sharpened claws and a big mouth with, it seemed, an abundance of oversized teeth. He had a cool, calm look of confidence on his face. He didn't just walk, he strolled. And he seldom ever looked to the left or to the right. But we didn't know there was anything really special about him until the day another cat came into the yard. Wamp chased him out immediately, and from then on he would allow no other cats around.

Then one day a big woods cat came in. These cats get very large, and they roam around quite a bit. But this big cat's experience was not to help him that day. Wamp met him in the yard. The big cat laid his ears back and began to growl. Wamp didn't believe in arguing. He went walking up to the cat sideways. When Wamp was about five or six feet from him, he made a dive for his head, grabbed him by the jaw with his teeth, and used his hind legs to claw his stomach. The big cat broke away and made for a clump of trees across the road and never stopped until he reached the top of a tree. Wamp, in hot pursuit, went right on up after him. The big cat jumped about thirty feet to the ground and kept going down a fencerow. Wamp knew he couldn't do that, so he backed down the tree and then down the fencerow he went. He was soon out of sight on the trail of the big cat, and there wasn't anything we could do to stop him. We didn't expect to see him again.

In about two hours, though, Wamp came walking up in the driveway. He looked somewhat messed up, but he still had his tail up and his head held high. He walked right on past us, not looking at anyone. He went to the kitchen door and stood there until someone let him in. He sat down by the refrigerator and waited. We gave him a little dish of hamburger and a saucer of milk. He still hadn't looked at anybody or paid anyone any mind. He had his own bed in a box in the house, and just before he went to his box, he turned and looked at me and winked. I swear it! You see, Wamp and I had a special kind of relationship. He knew that I knew that he was one helluva cat.

From that day on, Wamp really felt he owned the place. He treated us like visitors. He walked around in a kind of a prance, lifting his feet high with each step and holding his head to one side away from anyone who might be in view.

But Wamp had one weakness. He let our little girl, Betty, carry him around like a baby. He would lie on his back in her arms for as long as she would hold him. She had a doll buggy, and he allowed her to put him to bed with her doll. He would lie there with one paw around the doll and sleep for hours. One day after Betty had held him for some time, she put him down and found he had died.

Wampus was buried in style in a satin-lined shoe box under the big maple in the garden. We mourned his passing. Wamp was, as I said, one helluva cat!

Under the Influence

I have had a lot to say about my wife and our sons, but there is another chapter that must be written about our three lovely daughters. Some folks seemed to think that because our first three children were boys we would not be too impressed with the appearance on the scene of the girls. That was not and is not true at all. In fact, my whole life has been lived under the influence and guidance of women. A boy tells his troubles to his mother, of course. And when he has grown up and has met *the* girl, he discusses his plans for the future with her.

I was most fortunate as to my mother. She was wise and gentle, and at the same time she let us know, by setting a good example and with a few well-chosen words, that there were certain things we must not do. There was never a shadow of a doubt in our minds that she loved us. Then I grew up and met Bessie, and I was lucky again. As I've already said, I never understood why this gorgeous girl chose to marry me; how she managed to put up with me for fifty-three years, I will never know. She was honest and true; and when the chips were down, as I look back over the years, I don't recall that she ever came up with the wrong answer. I am sure there never was a more devoted mother. Then our three girls came along. They were good little girls and grew to be fine women. The oldest one, Ethel, married a masonry contractor. Our youngest girl, Betty, married a very talented radio broadcaster. That leaves the middle daughter, Cleo, who, up to now, is a career girl. She is a secretary at the U.S. Department of Agriculture's Forestry Sciences Laboratory on the Southern Illinois University campus at Carbondale.

The real pride and joy that came along with these little girls is difficult to put into words, but I'll try. A man comes in from a hard day's work in the fields, barn, and feedlot. He is tired, hot, and dirty. Things haven't gone too well that day. As he falls into the first chair he finds to relax for a few moments, a little girl—his own little girl—climbs up on his lap and snuggles up to him. She doesn't care that he is sweaty and dirty, and she looks at him as only a child can and tells him with that look and a shy little smile that he's the greatest. If that wouldn't melt the heart right out of a big lug, then he *is* a brute, not a man, and that's for sure.

Early to Rise

Of course, we were proud of our boys, too. It was quite an adventure watching them grow up to be big, strong men with ideas and ambition and the aggressiveness that is so necessary if one is to face up to this world—like men of days gone by who rose up early in the morning and went forth to do battle with the "tiger" with nothing but a club and a fifteen-cent Barlow knife as weapons and came home in the cool of the evening wearing a "tiger-skin coat" . . .

George

Lester

Wayne

Ethel

Charley

Cleo

Betty

The author's children

Afterword

Cleo Caraway

In 1971 the author, at age eighty-two, sold his farm—in his words, "one of the most difficult things I ever had to do"—and moved to Murphysboro. Dr. T. O. Miller is now the hand-picked ("he loves the land") owner of the author's home place and has built a new house on the site. The old house was moved intact to a neighboring farm.

The author had purchased his farm at age thirty-six. After forty-six years at the home place, the move to 2020 Herbert Street in Murphysboro was a traumatic experience for him, but he soon adjusted. His children, grandchildren, and great-grandchildren helped him settle in and were the continuing inspiration for his true stories and verbal essays on the state of the community, the nation, and the world. "And sometimes," he once said, "when I really get going, I even take in outer space."

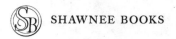 **SHAWNEE BOOKS**

Also available in this series . .